twenty something

ron lim

Copyright © 2024 Ron Lim

All rights reserved. No part of this book may be reproduced or used in any manner without written permission of the copyright owner except for the use of quotations in a book review.

For more information, please contact:
hello@ronwritings.com

ISBN: 978-981-94-1218-1

Independently Published by Ron Lim

Instagram: @ronwritings

ronwritings.com

chapters

1	a new beginning	4
2	into the unknown	38
3	stuck.	74
4	into the unknown (again)	114
5	a place in this world	144

a new beginning

twenty something

i am dedicating my twenties to this process.

i don't know what i'm going to do, but i'm going to figure it out.

i'll travel anywhere in the world. i'll hang out with anyone who is nice to me and is interesting. i'll try anything i haven't done before, as long as it excites me.

this is not a process where i will seek stability and find something to do on repeat. i'm here to get as much exposure as i can. there is so much to life. there are so many things i don't know.

i want to know more of what this life has to offer. i am dedicating my twenties to finding out as much as i can.

once i'm in my thirties, i will have all this exposure and it still won't be too late for me to settle. i'll then be able to decide what i should commit to.

this is my promise to myself.

twenty something

how boring it would be
to live a life
where you know exactly
what will happen
all the time

twenty something

how do you even begin
to get rid of the parts
you want to change?

and how do you
even explain
changing
when there is nothing wrong?

people
don't always understand it
we don't even understand it
ourselves

you feel miserable
but everything is fine
it doesn't feel so fine
but everything is fine

do you think
people are ever truly satisfied
or are they all just
pretending to be?

twenty something

how do you know
when what you have
is what you want?

i guess
we can never know
for sure

you have to decide
if you want change
or if you want things
to stay the same

it started off as an idea
a little thought
something i'd say to my friends
as a joke, sort of,
but also not really

i don't want to go to university
i would say,
i want to pack my bags and leave
go somewhere
and figure it out from there

i remember
it started out as a joke
a sassy remark
like how i'd always reply
something nonsensical
but secretly,
with a little truth in it

it all comes down to the moment
when it's time to make a decision
do you try to pull it off
or do you go with the flow
flowing where everyone goes?

you are caught up
in the wrong things
and you are aware of it

it's hard to change
when you are stuck
in the middle of it

you know what to do
but choices have consequences
you are not sure
if you are willing to deal with it
just yet

go with the flow
we all say
because it doesn't really make sense
to go against it

but where does
the flow take you
exactly?

drifting
drifting
drifting
drifting

you don't know where to stop
because you keep going with the flow
you keep ending up nowhere
because you keep going with the flow

do you really end up somewhere
if you keep drifting
or do you continue drifting
and drifting
and slowly
cease to exist

twenty something

if you don't show up
for yourself,
who will?

twenty something

there's more to life
than this shitty routine
you do on repeat

hanging out with people
you don't really care about
doing things
that don't light you up

there's more to it
there has to be

i believe
there is a version of life
out there
you will like more than this

you just have to find it
but you won't be able to
until you leave
what you don't like being in

you need to leave
you need to leave
you've probably told yourself this
countless times
but you are still here
what are you afraid of?

staying is easy
doing nothing is easy
so you stick with easy
and the funny thing is
you didn't even care about it
being easy in the first place

what are you afraid of?
you are afraid of change
but what is it about change
that scares you?

you don't know
but you are afraid
so you stay the same
so you stay the same

the most dangerous thing
is to live a life
never trying
because
you were too afraid to fail
so you choose to fail
by default

twenty something

you keep thinking
you have another go
and that is why
you never move forward

we fear change
we fear change
but what are we really afraid
of losing?

isn't it odd
how we want everything to change
but at the same time
we get so afraid
of changing?

things end
things end
fuck
they always end
and we stand there
wanting to move
but not knowing where to go

lately
i've been asking myself
which is scarier
is it really change
or is it things
staying the same?

twenty something

you can't live your life
not knowing what you want
telling people one thing
but craving for another

there is a difference between
being lost and being delusional
you can't expect to be happy
when you're chasing after
something you absolutely hate

you can't say that it's okay
when you don't feel okay
you can't say you're content
and secretly wish
for something else to happen

just because people are all
saying the same things
it doesn't mean that those things
are what you want too

what do you want?
you don't know
but you can begin
to find out

twenty something

if you think
you can do better,
then do it

you can spend a long time
waiting for something
and it can go away
in just a moment

when the opportunity
you have been waiting for
finally comes
do you take the risk
and wait a little longer,
or will you be ready
for change?

twenty something

i hope you find the courage
to do the things
you know you need to do
to grow

twenty something

how will you ever
get to where you want
if you think of one thing
but keep chasing another?

sometimes
we are blessed
to have more than one option
and it's funny
how that becomes a curse

have you ever been
in a situation
where you have two amazing options
and you end up doing
neither of them?

the opportunity is there
we see it
we see it
but we don't do it

the only thing we had to do
was to make a choice
but somehow
we still ended up
doing nothing

you don't always know what works better, but you know what you like more.

do what you like more.

if you like something more, you will do it more. and that will usually make it better.

if you like both equally, then it means you can do no wrong.

flip a coin. ask a friend. do whatever you need to do to make a choice.

if halfway through you realize you might like the other thing more, you can switch.

the worst thing you can do when caught between two excellent choices is to do nothing.

twenty something

you need to try things
or you will never
be able to find out
who you are

how can i
be here
when i also want
to be there?

you deserve better. you just have to allow yourself that.

you deserve people in your life that make you feel good.

you deserve people in your life that make you feel like you want to do good by them.

and trust that they will do the same for you in return.

leave if you feel like shit.

starting over is scary.

but being stuck in an eternal loop of something you dislike until you become what you dislike is even scarier.

is it strange
or are you just desperate
for a change?

down for anything
down for a good time
down to be feeling
a little less miserable

it didn't make sense before
and it still doesn't
things don't always have to
make sense

fuck that

you want things to change
you want it right away
you don't know what will happen
but something will happen

twenty something

if you are crazy enough
to believe
that you can,
you will

twenty something

it is the risks we take
that make us feel alive

twenty something

you are obsessed
with what you don't have
and that is the reason
why you don't feel alive

if there is someone
you are dying to talk to,
you should talk to them

if there is something
you want to do
and you can't stop thinking about it,
you should do it

record a podcast
write a book
start a vlog
or post your thoughts

if it works out
that is good
if it doesn't work out
you will stop thinking about it,
and that is also good

you have to let go of something that is okay to make room for something that is good.

it is hard to let go if you are uncertain.

but you will never find the certainty in something new until you let go of what you were holding onto before.

sometimes this ends up being a trap we get stuck in. holding onto something mediocre in hopes that something better will come along.

but it will never come. because we have no space for it.

and we end up waiting and waiting and eventually deciding that the mediocre thing we held onto was our best shot.

but it isn't.

the sad reality is that you end up settling for something less than what you want without ever giving the thing you want a proper shot.

twenty something

sometimes you just gotta say fuck it and go do whatever the heck you want to do

it took me a long time to be okay with leaving. it was an idea sitting in the back of my mind for years. festering. like an itch i couldn't scratch that never went away. i recognized i was unhappy and i felt like i had it in me to change. *if only my life was different. if only i had an opportunity.* i knew it wasn't going to come but a part of me kept wishing it would. if there is one thing i am grateful for, it is that i had that thought really young. i was probably 16 years old when i fully believed that my life was meant to be lived somewhere else. i didn't leave until i was 22. partly because i was afraid, but mostly because i had all these obligations that i had to fulfill. i think all those years of yearning made me radical. two weeks after i got my freedom, i bought a one way ticket and left. i realized the opportunity was already there. i spent years wishing i was free and i finally was. my life was right in front of me to do something with – if i wanted to. and i did.

it will probably end up being the best decision of my life.

and then it hits me

this is my life
i am still alive
and i can do whatever i want

so why am i stuck here
when i don't have to be?

into the unknown

the journey ahead
will be the longest journey
you've ever walked

this is the journey
where you become
the version of yourself
you were always meant to be

it will take time
to try things
and change your mind
about them

it will take time
to get over yourself
and firmly believe that
you are deserving
of whatever lies ahead

it will take time
to be consistent
especially on the days
you don't feel like it

the journey ahead
will be the longest journey
you've ever walked

there will be plenty of moments
your patience gets tested
there will be plenty of moments
you feel like stopping

but know this,
you can escape the effort
but you can never escape
the journey

some people
find themselves
within the shots they take

others
reach the end of their life
never giving it a proper shot

at the end of 2017, i was on a one-way flight to New Zealand. i was on my own, with a 6-month visa ahead of me, and 3 nights booked at a hostel in Auckland. i didn't know a thing about the country, didn't know anyone, and had no idea what i was going to do. in my mind, i was convinced that i could figure it out if i simply just showed up. that trip was a really big deal for me. my friends back home were just starting university. i knew if i took that trip, my life would never be linear to my friends' again. i had to make a life changing decision. stay on the path i've pursued my whole life, or leave and pursue the great unknown. i didn't know what the great unknown was going to be, but i knew i would never be happy staying. so i chose the latter. sitting alone on that 10-hour flight to New Zealand was when it finally sank in for me. *this is it. i'm doing it.* i don't know what i was expecting to feel. maybe a mixture of fear and anxiety. but it was neither of them. all i felt was relief. i felt like i was finally able to breathe. i felt all the weight that i had carried that didn't belong to me coming loose. it was the first time in my life i felt excitement for my future. it was on that flight that i knew for the first time, i made the right decision.

twenty something

it doesn't matter
where you start
it will all lead you
to the same place

stop saving your opportunities until you don't have them anymore. we wait and wait for the best time to do something, but it never is the best time. so we end up waiting and waiting. and the opportunity you were sitting on did not get bigger. you just become more and more depleted while you wait. you see people taking a shot and you see some of them make it. and you hate yourself for not trying. but the opportunity is still there. but you still don't feel ready for it. so you continue to wait. and there will come a day where you completely lose interest in it and just don't have the desire to do it anymore. or you find out that enough people have gotten onto it and it doesn't work anymore. so you look for the next opportunity. and the cycle repeats.

your twenties is the best time to try things.

you just got your freedom. there is a whole life ahead of you.

you can do anything you want, but you don't know where to begin.

here's the thing – you can begin anywhere. it doesn't matter where. it matters that you begin.

start anywhere, and you will find your way to where you're meant to be.

you have a fire in you. keep that fire burning by doing things that make you feel alive. don't let your flame burn out because you listen too much to others and not enough to yourself.

make mistakes. this is the time where you can fuck up the most and suffer the least consequences. the more mistakes you make, the more clarity you will gain.

it will never be too late to settle. let yourself live a little.

put it out
you can always delete it
if you don't like it

say hi first
you can always walk away
if they don't say it back

make a change
you can always revert
if you change your mind

be nice first
you can always move on
if it's not reciprocated

the point is
you always have the next move
if you want it
you can make it

the next time
you find yourself waiting
for too long,
that is something for you
to think about

twenty something

the more you let go
the more you can become

twenty something

the only person
stopping you
is you

things i've learned in my twenties:

1. stop waiting for the perfect time. the perfect time is when you start.
2. don't take risks you don't believe in.
3. learn to do things alone. if you always wait for other people, you'll miss out on a lot.
4. if you can't beat fear, just do it scared.
5. if you don't sacrifice for what you want, what you want becomes the sacrifice.

don't play it safe.

it's too early to have it figured out.

you don't even know what's out there, and you're already trying to find something to commit to.

what you need right now isn't an answer, it's more exposure.

nothing really stands out because you haven't found the thing that's meant for you yet.

you need to take risks. you need to try things that make you excited.

but you're too focused on playing it safe and convincing yourself that sensibility is good for you.

you still have so much time ahead of you.

there will be plenty of time in the future to play it safe.

don't settle before your life has even begun.

your twenties are the craziest years of your life. some of your friends are still in school. some of your friends are married. some of your friends have a completely different life. some of your friends are still the exact same person. some of your friends are not your friends anymore. you had to live a certain way all your life and suddenly, your life can be whatever you want. everything in your twenties will change. you will meet people. you will lose people. you will try plenty of things you haven't before. and you will fail at most of them. you will feel lost. oh yes, you will feel lost all the time. but you will grow through them. and you will become a better person for it. let your twenties be wild. let your twenties be crazy. let yourself be introduced to a life you don't know about yet. and most importantly – let yourself have fun in the process.

try everything.

listen to opinions but make your own decisions.

don't settle unless it's something you really really really want.

don't get hung up on failures, you don't have to make it right now.

this phase is all about exposure. do that for a few years and everything in life will become much clearer.

people will try to tell you things based on their experience.

but they don't know anything.

everything they know is subjective.

they don't know who you are, they don't know what you've been through, they don't know what you want.

they tell you they tried for their dreams and it didn't work out and they gave up. and they discourage you from chasing yours.

but they don't know what will happen. you don't know what will happen.

there are many things you need to try out for yourself.

even if it doesn't work out, there is something for you to learn in the process. and that lesson might be what you need to make it further in the future.

follow your intuition, and don't do anything you're not convinced of.

twenty something

i think growth
is meant to be
confusing,
because
if you're not questioning
then how
are you finding out?

twenty something

nothing will
hold you back
like the weight of
what you are avoiding

let people talk shit about you.

it doesn't matter what they say. it is not important.

focus on where you are and where you are trying to be. everything else is irrelevant.

people don't understand what you want. people don't know what you've been through.

if they wanted to know, they would ask. if they didn't ask, it probably means they don't care.

and if they don't care about you, you don't need to care about them.

these are people who won't be in your life for too long anyway.

the funny thing is – the narrative will change when you get to where you want to be. but you can't get to where you want to be if you let these irrelevant opinions affect you.

keep focusing on yourself and doing what you know you gotta do. everything else will align after.

it's crazy how quickly
the wrong people
can drain the energy
out of you

twenty something

you don't know them
and they don't know you
why are you so concerned
with what they think
about you?

twenty something

some days are easy
and some other days
we make it hard
for ourselves

you are the only person
trying to stop yourself
and sometimes,
you are not sure why

the things you do
and the things you don't
it's all on you
it's all on you

we look for an answer
when there is no answer
we try to explain
when there is no need to explain

is it a hard life
or are you making it hard
for yourself?

twenty something
without a clue
on what we should do

twenty something
with a burning desire
to make something happen

twenty something
they say we're lost
so they tell us where we belong

twenty something
are we really lost
if we don't care where we go

twenty something
fuck your expectations
we will make our own

twenty something

you are the main character
of your own story
but you are too busy
living in someone else's

how good could you be if you actually gave a shit about what you are doing?

stop explaining yourself.

it doesn't matter. just do things. you don't need to convince anyone else but yourself.

you don't need to justify any of your choices as long as they make sense to you.

the person living the consequences of your actions is you.

it doesn't matter what others say or think. you need to be okay with your decisions.

this life is yours and you choose your own life. what we choose is what we get.

it's better this way.

the alternative is you living a life that isn't yours. you give in to opinions you don't agree with and you get a life that you don't want.

it's better this way.

twenty something

it's funny
when you think of your life
like a video game
you realize that
it's not so different after all

you can go anywhere you want
you can talk to whomever you want
you can jump around
be stupid
people will look at you
and none of it will matter

it's funny
because in a video game
you don't care
you are just there to have fun

but somehow
in real life
you have all these barriers
to restrict yourself
you stop yourself from having fun
but you don't know why
but you don't know why

twenty something

is life complicated
or do we make it more
than it should be?

my problem is
i have a good idea
and a good desire

but i overthink
and i feel like
i have to be better
than what i currently am

so i go on a journey
to be better
and better
but it's never enough
it's never enough for me

depleted
and defeated
i lose my desire
so i give up on my good idea

reality is
none of that even mattered
it was good at the start
it was good in the middle

i stopped myself
before i'd even begun

this year
i hope you find the thing
that you have been
searching so hard for

and if not,
i hope you find the courage
to begin your search

we spend so much time
doubting ourselves
that we forget
what we want

the person making your life complicated is you. you want things to be a certain way, but you don't always want to put in the work to get there. you hope for an opportunity to change your life but when you find it, you turn it down because it didn't look the way you want it to be. as a whole, there are no real problems with your life. but you find yourself trying to put out fires all the time. you reject "better" in hopes of finding the "best", but nothing is ever good enough for you. sometimes you wonder if life would be simpler if you weren't so "smart". but the funny thing is – life is already simple. it always has been. you just have to let it be.

it's hard to change
until you do it
then it's hard
to change back

you talk yourself out of
the things you want the most
the only person
standing in your way
is you

we care too much
about missing our shot
and too little
about shooting it

life feels confusing
but it keeps flowing
you are waiting
for something to come
but you need to create it

twenty something

you are here
but you wish to be there

life is a twisted contradiction
of getting to where you want to be
and wishing that
you were somewhere else again

twenty something

i remember
when i was younger
all i wanted
was to grow up
and figure it out

i remember
spending a lot
of my teenage years
wishing i was older
and finally be done
with this lame routine

i remember
growing older
feeling excited
but also scared,
what if it doesn't work out?

i remember
when all i ever wanted to do
was to leave everything behind
do it all again
somewhere new,
somewhere else

i remember
leaving.
so liberated,
feeling exhilarated
ready to take on the world

i remember
i remember it all
it feels like i've come so far
but also barely at all

i remember
wanting to be here
and now that i am here
why does it still
somewhat
feel the same?

stuck.

twenty something

a new phase
another new beginning
it feels like life has been
changing around a lot lately

i know
i talk about figuring it out a lot
but what does "out" mean?
is there ever an out?
or do we just keep figuring?

it's not always easy
going through it alone
i find myself getting stuck a lot
with everywhere to go
but nowhere to call home

leaving was never easy
until you left
and now
it's the easiest thing ever

so easy
to pack your bag and go
but the question is
where do you put it down again?

twenty something

i want to be simpler
and i also want
to be more

you have a fixed notion
of how the world
is supposed to work
and that is what restricts you

you don't know what you want
so you chase after
what someone else wants
thinking
maybe you will like it too

the irony comes
when the person you tried to model
had no idea what they wanted
it was a false pretense,
and you find yourself
chasing after a fraud

if it went on
for a little longer
would it have made
any difference?

sometimes
you're forced to make decisions
in a split moment
but you never really know
what to choose

we walk away
from things
and we think about
walking back to it

did it not work out
because you didn't do enough
or was it simply
not meant for you?

you leave
and you come back
and it's not really
the same

the friend group
you used to hang with
is now disbanded

your best friend
has a new partner
you've never met before

your room
looks exactly the same
but the sense of belonging
is gone

what used to be your world
now barely feels like
it holds much significance
at all

where do you go
when home
doesn't feel like home
anymore?

twenty something

some of us get lost in the chaos
some of us find ourselves in it

twenty something

do you ever wonder
if the thing
you are looking forward to
will ever come true
or will you just keep
looking forward to it?

they tell us to wait
they tell us to be patient
i don't know,
sitting here and waiting
doesn't feel like
it's getting any closer

is this a process
or is this a joke
do you move higher
or do you come back
to the same circle?

isn't it funny
how the same expectation
can kill you
over and over again?

most of the time
the answer you are looking for
is right in front of you

and most of the time
you are too busy looking for it
everywhere else

it can't be that easy
you say,
as you proceed to make your life
more difficult for yourself

twenty something

the longer you wait
the less likely
you will do it

it's the empty promises
it's the disappointments
it's the desperation
that makes you go
fuck it
and embark on a journey
entirely on your own

if you can't relate to this
you are *lucky*

you will never have to
deal with the pressure
of making it on your own
while everyone else
is watching you
secretly hoping for you to fail

you will never have to
hear your thoughts
simultaneously screaming at you
when you're in a foreign place
in an empty room
alone
knowing that there is no way out
unless you figure this out
on your own

twenty something

you will never have to
know the feeling
of looking at someone
and having absolute certainty
that nothing they say can be trusted
because people are unreliable
because no one is on
the same wavelength as you
and no matter what they tell you
you will still eventually end up alone
because you can't make someone
be accountable for themselves
if they are not ready for it

you will never have to
look back at all you've done
the bittersweetness
of the whole process
a taste you never quite forget
and be like *wow*
i really did all that
on my own?

if you can't relate to this
you are *lucky*
but if you think about it
are you, really?

twenty something

it is the
disappointments
that make you
an independent person

twenty something

stop saying
i don't care
when you actually
really do

there is so much
you can do in this life
but it is hard to see that
when you are
surrounded by people
on a different wavelength
to you

all you need is one friend to change your life. someone you can really just be yourself with. someone who doesn't say "you've changed" but rather, encourages you to try new things and experiment with different ways of being. someone you can say everything and anything to. someone who knows that deep down you're a good person, so they won't judge you when you say something wrong because they understand you aren't always good at expressing what you think. all you need is that one friend who will be your pillar of support as you're navigating through change, and you will never feel out of place throughout the process.

there are people
you can be with every moment
and your energy
never seems to run out

and there are people
who deplete you completely
despite you feeling like
you haven't done much

the most dangerous thing
is when the first type of person
becomes the second
but you're too hung up on the past
to make a change

people are everything. the right ones will make you feel like there is nothing missing from your life, and the wrong ones will leave you feeling empty all the time. we become the people we surround ourselves with. your life will look similarly to the person you see everyday. you will do the same things. you will think the same way. you will believe in the same possibilities, and you will share similar doubts and fears. if you ever find yourself in a situation where you are around the wrong people, i hope you find the courage to begin again. the right people will make a difference. the right people will be worth resetting for.

you feel stuck
but at the same time
there are so many things
you can choose

too many options
you can't decide
sometimes
you just gotta pick one
without knowing
what will happen

and maybe
that's how you begin

pick something
anything
go from there
and change it again
when you have to

most answers
are usually simple

if you're overthinking,
it's too complicated

it's funny how we think we're running out of time
when in reality, the real part of our lives hasn't
even started

there are a few more things
that need to happen
for you to get to
where you want to be

young one
you need patience
patience is not waiting
patience is you continuing

you want something
and you realize that
you can't have it right away
so you give it up

you pursue something else
something completely irrelevant
something you don't care about
because you can't have
the thing that you want

you can't have it right away
you can't have it right now
so you give it up
so you give it up

the process to "figure it out" is going to take an overwhelmingly long amount of time. there is so much that goes into trial and error that is not talked about. you start off with a completely clean slate. your life can be anything you want, but what will it be? and how will you do it? it's hard to know what to do when you don't know what you want. the key is to keep trying and trying and trying. you can't be reluctant to make decisions because that's all you will be doing. one decision after another after another. in hopes that one of them will finally be what you want. the chase is mostly intuitive. you're going after a feeling, and you can't know how you will feel until you have it. one way or another, you will get to where you want to be. but only if you never stop trying.

twenty something

it can always
be better
and it can always
be worse

where you are
is enough
whenever you decide
that it is

do you ever have days
where it's hard to show up
your mind feels overloaded
your soul feels exhausted
there is this
deep
weight
resting upon you
and you can't seem to shake it off

you're scrolling too much
you're forgetting your meals
everything you do
seems to make you more lethargic
you want to call the day forfeit
but you can't keep making that call

do you ever have days
where it's hard to show up
you want this slump to be over
but you keep giving in to
the first distraction that comes along
one more scroll
ten more minutes
alright i'll do this in an hour
alright
one more hour

twenty something

you know you're better than this
but right now it's got the better of you
you're learning it the hard way
most things are easier said than done
the only lie you tell yourself is
i can start anytime i want

do you ever have days
where it's hard to show up
except that this time
you show up anyway

you make your bed
you cook your food
you sit down at the table
and you do what you gotta do
despite how little you feel like it

you're learning it the hard way
that nothing is tougher than your grit
pure willpower triumphs over
any excuses you might have
and once you're through with that,
it feels good to beat it
oh man
does it feels good
to beat it

the first time i went back home after solo traveling, i was utterly miserable. i had just spent the past few months having the best experience of my life. it was strange going from every day being an unknown to every day being completely the same. it was strange to come back and see that nothing had changed at all. my friends were still living the same life, complaining about the same things, and wishing that they could be somewhere else. it felt like i went back in time and that whole trip i did was a dream. i think something about that moment fucked with my head a little bit. it made me realize how quickly things could change if we let them. it made me realize how much power we hold over our own lives. i was unhappy before i left, and i got even more unhappy after i came back. now that i got a little taste of what leaving meant, it was really hard for me to stay.

there is a certain kind of calm
in melancholy
knowing things are not okay
but they will be,
eventually

twenty something

somewhere
in the middle now
and i don't know
where this is going

but if the alternative
is me not moving
i guess i don't have a choice
but to keep on going

someone will find you
something will find you
i don't know if it's true
but what other choice
do i have, really?

if i knew
i would get myself
into this whole complicated mess
i would do it all again,
gladly

"what will happen if you don't give up?"

probably everything.

lately i've been feeling like
everything i do
comes back
to the same lesson

do the things
you say you will
it is as simple
and as difficult as that

we overthink
and talk ourselves
out of situations
we shouldn't get out of

things are tough
until they aren't
we try to get ahead of ourselves
and it comes back to bite us
every single time

twenty something

it takes time
to become someone
you haven't been before

twenty something

some day
you will look back
and it will all be
fucking amazing

it probably doesn't
seem like it right now
you're counting down
to the next countdown
to the next countdown

always looking forward
to the future
never enjoying the present

you are excited
for the next phase of life
to come along
only to find yourself
wishing it would be over
once you are in it

there are days
where you are not sure
what the whole purpose
of doing this is

twenty something

you are so tempted
to fuck it up
throw it all away
and you know what
you probably could
you probably could

it's hard to see it now
but there has to be an end to this
this journey can't last forever
you will come to a point
where you either reach your expectation
or you change it

keep going
keep going
keep going
whatever you do,
just keep going

some day
you will look back
and it will all be
fucking amazing

the biggest things happen in the smallest ways. your new best friend could've been that girl who was sitting next to you at the cafe last week who looked like she really wanted someone to talk to. if only you said hi. all that poetry you wrote in your notes app when you were really heartbroken could have been a bestselling book. if only you had put it out. that two-week solo trip to Bali could have been the inspiration behind you moving to a new place. if only you didn't talk yourself out of booking it. the thing is – opportunity comes out of nowhere and everywhere. you are always one step away from your life completely changing. don't let the abundance of opportunities be the reason why your life continues to remain at a standstill.

things i've learned in my twenties:
1. talk to strangers. it will change your life.
2. if something doesn't work out, change the plan, not the goal.
3. if you can't control it, embrace it.
4. try things out for yourself. that's how you find out the "real" answer.
5. if you're confused, the answer is probably no.

twenty something

forget everything you're used to.

you don't want the things you wanted in the past. you want what you want now.

but you're not letting yourself have what you want.

maybe because it contradicts a certain self-belief you've had in the past.

or maybe you've already spent so much time committing to this other thing and you don't want to "waste" all the time you've put in.

but it's funny. because your solution to not waste time is to waste more time.

forget about what you're used to for a minute. focus on now.

what do you want now?

your past is over. your future is coming.

don't fuck up your future for something that has already passed.

twenty something

i am too far gone
to go back to
where i came from

it might be easier
to just keep heading
into the unknown

into the unknown
(again)

here we go again
i'm finding myself
in a different country

back into the unknown
starting over
trying again

the plan is
to figure out a plan
as always

start somewhere
and hope that
it leads to somewhere else

it doesn't always work out
but you can always
try again
and again

i don't remember
how many times
i have done this

each time
i start over
i think i might be
getting a little better

twenty something

i feel like
i have the pieces i need
but i am struggling
to piece it all together

twenty something

uncertainty is a great thing
there is hope in the unknown
maybe
it will turn out better
than you think

mistakes are a great thing
you can only do it once
and you will remember
never to do it again

betrayals are a great thing
they save you time
from figuring out
who the wrong ones are

there is good in every bad
something can only hurt you
as much as you let it
every obstacle you go through now
will only make the future smoother

you live and you learn
it is the fastest way
for your life to become great

we want something. and we want it right away.
but it doesn't always work like that.

we get ideas. and we get excited. we want it to
happen. and we want it to happen right now.

there is an entire process to get from where we are
to where we want to be. and sometimes we
disregard that completely. despite us being fully
aware of it.

sometimes things don't work out for a long time.
despite you being consistent and applying a lot of
effort into it.

and then it does. when it does, it happens all at
once.

i think a lot of us are one thing away from having
our lives completely changed. i don't know what
that thing is. but all it takes is one.

the only thing to do is to keep trying. and maybe
one day something you do will click. and things
will start moving up from there.

it's better to
have lived a life
with a few mistakes made
but where you can proudly say
you were happy with what you got

most people have a life
avoiding all mistakes
they can say that they've never failed
but they have also never
lived a life at all

some day
i hope all of this
will somewhat
make sense

don't ever let anyone who gave up on their dreams convince you to give up on yours. don't ever let anyone who has never shown up for themselves convince you that it's not worth taking a shot. don't ever let anyone convince you to give up before you even try. your path ahead does not have to look like everyone else's. you can give in to what people around you think is best for you to do, or you can at least make an attempt towards what you want. even if it doesn't work out, at least you know better. you still have a long way ahead, and there is plenty of room for mistakes. don't give up before you even begin.

twenty something

the best thing
you can do for your life
is to do the things
you say you will

you don't need to worry about what the path ahead will be before you reach it.

all you have to do is to keep moving.

the worst thing you can do is to over question yourself and stop when you don't need to stop.

everything you are doing is working out for the greater good.

the only way you can fail is if you stop.

twenty something

as i sit here
with my coffee
and think about the future ahead
filled with uncertainties

there is nothing
but excitement
thinking about how much better
my life can become

live on the road
work on the road
make enough money on the road
so i can keep living on the road

there is no need to go home
when the whole world is your home
i'll keep doing this
until i run out of money
or until i find a new home

maybe i am lucky because i didn't come from much. maybe i am lucky because i don't really miss home whenever i am gone. maybe i am lucky because taking my first step out is already better than what my life used to be. maybe that's the reason why it's so easy for me to keep going. maybe that's the reason why i keep looking forward, because there's nothing much for me to look back to. and maybe that's the reason why it will end up working out for me. maybe without realizing it, that was exactly the kind of luck i needed.

twenty something

you can be
really grateful
for where you are in life
and still want more
for yourself

there are people you meet for the first time and your souls immediately recognize each other. you listen to them talk and you can't help smiling to yourself. you hear things you've been thinking about but never said out loud, and it's relieving to know you're not the only one. you don't know anything about them, but something about their presence just feels familiar to you. it's like listening to a song for the first time and immediately knowing that this will be one you'll play on repeat. you leave the meet up without making future plans, but something in the air tells you that you will definitely see each other again.

things take time to work
i am trying to remind myself of that

we try something for the first time
and we get an impulsive urge
to want to see results right away

i wish it worked that way
but we are not always
immediately capable
it takes time
it takes time

things take time to work
often more than we think
it doesn't mean your ideas suck
or your execution is shit
sometimes you just need more time

i am writing this to remind myself
that things take time to work
be patient
keep doing the things
you know you gotta do
and life will work out
and life will work out

twenty something

people will give you all sorts of advice.

most of it won't work. because they are not you.

they don't know what you want.

they will tell you to chase after things that worked for them, but they don't understand that you might not want the same thing.

it doesn't mean that their advice is wrong, it just means that it's not for you.

but people will spend an unnecessary amount of time trying to prove that their advice actually "works".

and it does. but the point isn't just trying to find one that works. you also want it to make you happy.

it doesn't "work" if you end up being miserable in the process.

twenty something

the biggest mistake you can make

is to wait when you're already fully capable of doing it yourself.

stop waiting for people to come. stop waiting for your friends to be ready.

if you were meant to do it with someone, you would have found them by now.

some things are meant for you to do alone. the most important things usually are.

you don't need someone. you want someone. there is a difference.

if you keep waiting for your conditions to be perfect before you begin, you will never begin.

if there is something you really want to achieve, do it on your own first.

elevate yourself and your energy. the rest will come.

maybe this chapter of your life is meant for you to do it alone. maybe this is the time for you to practice independence – to do the things you've always known but kept putting off for some reason. maybe this phase is meant for you to be a little bored and lonely. maybe this is what you need as you're putting your pieces back together. maybe it won't be fun, but it is necessary. maybe this is what you need to go through to evolve into the next version of yourself.

stop wasting your time on people who are not at the same pace as you. people are either ready or they aren't. most people aren't ready. most people have shit they gotta go through before they are ready. most people are not as desperate as you. how much time have you wasted when you had the energy and excitement to do something but you held yourself back because you were waiting for someone else to be ready to do it with you? and they are never fucking ready. or they do things half-heartedly and they pull out the moment it gets difficult. and you lose all your energy in the process. stop wasting your own time. find people on your level. or fucking do it alone if you have to.

the biggest lesson i need to learn now

is to just create the things i want to happen by myself.

maybe there will be people who will join me on my journey. maybe there won't.

i'm tired of people who do things half-heartedly or are still indecisive about their own life choices.

i'm tired of waiting.

i don't even know what i'm waiting for. it's becoming a distraction at this point.

i know what i want to happen and i know how to make those things happen.

i just need to do it.

my definition of fun has changed over the years. staying at home on a Saturday night cooking dinner and putting on a film is more exciting than going to a nightclub and trying to talk to people i don't know. making myself go to the gym even when i don't feel like it and i never regret that workout. working on my business is fun. figuring out the things i need to do better and seeing the growth is super exciting. over the years, i've found a lot of enjoyment being alone and it's easy for me to say no now if i don't feel like doing something. i no longer hang out with people who don't make me feel good because there is literally no reason to. life seems to be getting better and i'm also finding myself enjoying it more at the same time. i used to think that these two things come at the expense of the other, and it's been great learning that it doesn't have to be that way.

twenty something

i'm not there yet
not even close
i don't even know
where "there" is
or what it means

different people
have different life paths
some people do more
and some people are happy
without doing too much

your start
could be the goal for some people
and the conventional goal
might not be something
you care about at all

life is a personal process
how involved
do you want to be?

you can spend a long time looking for answers but it won't change anything when you finally find them.

when you find the answer, that is only the beginning.

then you need to begin on a journey to do all the things you know you need to do.

it is the doing that makes the difference, not the knowing.

we all know that. but most of us continue to look for more answers, despite knowing that it won't make a difference.

twenty something

if you never take a risk
your life will never change

my superpower in life is that i truly believe i can achieve everything i want on my own. i can't think of a specific person or thing i'm reliant on anymore. i survived for a long time on my own and i am slowly learning how to thrive. i am by no means where i want to be yet, but i believe i'm at a point in my life now where things can only get better. if i covered all the distance i've made so far on my own, the road ahead can only be easier. this is not to say that i am choosing to be alone moving forward. i'm not. i love people. but good people are not always easy to find. and i've been through enough people now to know that finding new people is the easy part. finding someone you want to stay with and for them to also want it is the difficult part. and i'd rather be alone now than to be with people i know i'll eventually be disappointed by.

twenty something

the moment i realized
what i could do with my own life
i stopped being so caught up
with what others were doing

most things
are irrelevant to me
most people
are not on the same path as me

what i want to have,
i have to create
it doesn't matter what others are doing
it doesn't change anything for me

the moment i realized
what i could do with my life
was the moment i had to decide
if i wanted to go for it
or watch it pass me by

twenty something

i don't know if you know
but nothing really scares me anymore
the demons in my head
they are now my friends

i've lived in dark places
and made a home out of it
i've learned how to let the light in
but i still like to keep it dark sometimes

the monsters under my bed
are now standing guard by the door
there is nothing you can say to me
that i haven't said to myself before

my biggest fear
remains to be myself

maybe
what i'm actually afraid of
are the things i can do
if i allow myself
to really try

twenty something

i don't know where
i'm going to end up
but i'm on my way
to find out

a place in this world

twenty something

there is a shift happening.

things are slowing down. coming to an end.

phase change. moving out from the past and into a future that you will create.

everything ahead is unknown. and you are slowly starting to be okay with that.

people you are unfamiliar with. things you haven't done before.

you don't know anything, but you know this. you want more. and it has never felt more within your grasp than this moment.

there is still a gap between where you are and where you want to be. but you know it's possible now.

it's up to you if you are willing to close that distance.

it scares you but it also excites you. that is your sign to keep going.

twenty something

how do you know
where to go
when you can go
anywhere?

how do you know
what to do
when you can do
anything?

how do you know
whom to be with
when you can be with
anyone?

i don't know
what i'm searching for
but i think i will know
when i find it

all i'm looking for is
a place in this world
somewhere i can be in
and not feel like
i want to be
somewhere else

twenty something

my goals are big
but they are realistic to me
i don't care if no one believes it
i'm on my way to get it

most people talk about things
very few actually go after it
the life i want
will be unfathomable to you
my belief is blind naivety
but i know it will come true

if you spend your entire life
trying to make one thing happen
there is no way
it won't happen

i've seen the ending
i've decided my fate
the road ahead is unpredictable
but the outcome is sealed
one way or another
i will find my way to it

twenty something

it is what you do
with what you know
that changes
everything

people use the words
you have changed
like it's some kind of insult,
but is it really?

to them
i would say thank you,
kindly

if you didn't like the person
you were before
and you change that
isn't that what you'd call
growth?

twenty something

trying to be
a little comfortable
with the things that
make me uncomfortable
so i can be a little better

luck is a funny word.

when i was 7,
i remember seeing someone
play the piano on tv
and i remember
being so captivated

i told my mom
i would love to learn it
she said to me
we have no money
go learn it yourself when you get older

when i was 13,
i heard someone at school
talk about their trip to Australia
i went back home and told my mom
i'd love to go to Australia
sweet boy
she said to me
even i have never been to Australia
one day
when you are old enough
you will be able to do it

twenty something

when i was 18,
i saved all the money i had
and i got my driver's license
it was probably my biggest achievement yet
and i said to my dad
wouldn't it be nice
if i had a car to drive
me too
said my dad
me too

when i was 22,
i left behind
all the friends i'd made since i was 7
i left behind
every single family member
i was ready for a change
and i wasn't just talking about it

i scraped every penny i had
took it all with me
invested it in a solo travel trip
and never looked back

you know what i mean
when i say that
luck is a funny word
because i was told growing up
that i wasn't so lucky like everyone else
and if i ever wanted anything
i had to get it on my own

the funny thing is
the moment i did that
all i hear is
how does he do it
he is so lucky
and i never quite comprehended
the kind of luck they meant

luck
doesn't mean anything to me
i didn't have it at the beginning
i don't need it now

some people do things
some people look at the people
who do things
and think about
how lucky they are

twenty something

you know you've found your place when you are
no longer trying to escape from it

twenty something

not everything
has to make sense
to everyone

happiness
isn't always logical

if it makes you happy
and doesn't hurt anyone,
stop worrying about
justifying your actions
to others

nothing is more inspiring than your own efforts. seeing the work you put in come to fruition. perhaps it's the gains you get from hitting the gym. perhaps it's your self-published book finally getting some traction. perhaps it's that soccer ball you bought 5 days ago and played with for an hour a day and now for the first time in your life, you are able to kick a ball. it is always a pleasant surprise how quickly we improve when we really put our hearts into something. you realize that you've always been able to do that thing, but for some reason always talked yourself out of it. there is this newfound motivation to want to get better when you see yourself improve for the first time. but there is also this slight inclination to want to sit back down on our asses. we don't always succeed at fighting back that inclination. and sometimes, we give up even when things are going well. it makes no sense, but we still give in to it. we are the best at inspiring ourselves, but we are also the best at self-sabotaging. which is why i love this game. it is truly a race against yourself. the only person you need to beat is your old self. and the only thing you need is simply willpower.

the people you hang around with truly matters.

energy is so infectious. you become what you're exposed to.

having pleasant people around you will make you a more pleasant person.

and if people around you are bitter, you will become bitter.

i know it's hard to find good people when you don't have good people.

there are phases in our lives where we know we are in a toxic situation, but the fear of starting over is so great that you try to justify the toxicity instead.

you tell yourself things like "it could be worse", as if that makes your situation better.

no.

just because it could be worse, doesn't mean it has to suck.

twenty something

spend time with others
and spend time with yourself
notice which version of you
you enjoy more

that will tell you
what you need to know
about the people
you hang around with

twenty something

i don't want to be a nice person
i don't want to be the guy
people come to when they need something
and leave hanging
once they get what they want

i don't want to be a nice person
the person that has to do things
with no expectations
it's a nice feeling to be reciprocated
i don't want to miss out on that

i don't want to be a nice person
i know when the time to say no is
but it's hard to be the person
who disappoints
when you've lived a life full of disappointments

when i say that
i don't want to be a nice person
what i really mean is that
i don't want to be taken advantage of

i want a life
where you are nice
and the people you are with
are also nice to you
and i refuse to settle
for anything less than that

twenty something

be mindful
of your own energy

observe how it changes
when you are around different people
being in different spaces
doing different things

if it makes you feel good
keep it close
if you feel like shit
let it go

tune your energy
by holding on and letting go
of different things you come across

when there is no longer a moment
you feel like you want to escape from
that will be the beginning of your journey
towards abundance

being able to make
your own decisions
is a *superpower*

most people let others
decide their lives
for them

twenty something

find your intuition
and then follow it
you won't always get
what you want
but it will bring you to exactly
where you're meant to be

here is why it is important to be yourself.

think about it.

if you pretend to be someone you are not, and you end up being liked for it, it is not a good thing.

eventually you will get exposed, or you will get sick of pretending, and you will lose everything you've built.

if someone doesn't like you as you are, it is a good thing.

it saves you time from forming a relationship, only to realize down the road, that you are incompatible.

if you are yourself and someone likes you for it, you know they are a real one.

you will never worry about how you should be or question if the other person is being genuine with you.

be yourself. it will save you a lot of time.

i don't know how to be happy when i'm not.

i can't fake it.

i hear people talk about "fake it till you make it" all the time, but it doesn't work like that for me.

maybe it's something i haven't learned to do, or maybe my brain is wired too practically that i can't see a situation other than how it is.

the thing is – i also don't know if i want to pretend to be happy when i'm not.

i like the periods where things suck and i have to figure out how to get out of it.

and i like the periods where i figured it out and i get to enjoy for a little bit.

the ebbs and flows are part of the process. and i believe they all lead me to where i'm eventually meant to be.

i wouldn't want to jeopardize the process by pretending to be someone i've not yet become.

twenty something

i know
it can be annoying
when someone says something
that just isn't right
and you feel a need to correct them

but the truth is
there are these people
who don't care about being right
they just like to criticize
and it makes them feel good
putting other people down

you can't let these
energy vampires
put you down
they don't care about you
and you shouldn't care about them either

you don't have to react to
everything you notice
let them say what they want
you know what's right
and they will always have shit to say
about something
anyway

your energy is the most precious thing you have. watch who you spend it on. watch what you spend it on. if you hang around people who do not inspire you, you start to become skeptical of all things good. if you keep doing things that do not uplift you, you start to feel like shit. over time, your energy to want to do something becomes lesser and lesser, and you start finding everything "too tiring" to do. you become the kind of person who would rather spend their time trying to kill time than do something meaningful with it. protect your energy. if you give it to something shitty, you're going to get shit back in return.

sometimes i wonder what my life would have been like if i had never left. would i have become the person i am today? i would probably still be stuck thinking about all the things i have now done. i would still be afraid, making up situations i don't really believe and being crippled by irrational fear. i would still be envious, looking at people on the internet living their best lives and thinking about how unlucky i am. i might have done some traveling, but i would never have gotten to know the world. i wouldn't know what it feels like to sit at the Donaukanal in Vienna with a beer on a sunny day. i wouldn't know the feeling of driving through the Canggu shortcut in Bali with a scooter watching people almost fall into rice fields. nor would i have enjoyed a Fergburger in Queenstown, New Zealand with four friends i just met a week prior on a bus. i would have seen people living in other countries, but i would have never known their stories. if i had never left, i imagine my life would be exactly the same. and now that i have lived the life i have, i can't imagine a life being deprived of all of that.

happiness
is really just
a bunch of simple things
on repeat
over and over again

i've never really
prided myself as being tough
i like my life to be easy
if there was an easy way out
i'd take it
every single time

i do however
pride myself in getting things done
i try to be
a man of my word
and if i can't be accountable to myself
who else
can i be accountable to?

how you do one thing
is how you do everything
sometimes there's an easy way
sometimes there is just the way
either way
easy doesn't mean a thing
if you don't get it done
i try to live by that

i'm not tough
but i am intentional
if i want something
i don't stop
until i get it done

things i've learned in my twenties:
1. if it makes you happy, it's good enough.
2. don't settle for less because you are too impatient to wait for the best.
3. it is easy to repeat something 10 times. repeating it 1000 times is what makes a difference.
4. good things are simple. if it's starting to feel complicated, find your way back.
5. just have some fun. most things are not that deep.

twenty something

i don't really want
the things i used to want
anymore

i don't really want
the people i used to want
the people i craved for
or the people
who didn't want me back

i've restarted my life
more times than i can count now
new place
new people
i know i can always
begin again

what's gone is gone
i don't need it
there is still plenty ahead
and i know somewhere within it
there is something
for me

plant your seeds
grow your flowers
be careful
who you let into your garden

welcome the ones
who water your plants
chase away the people
who step on your flowers

your mind is your garden
give it light and water
cut away the weeds
and watch your life
slowly bloom

twenty and twenty one
i know the life i have isn't the life i want
man i am so ready to run
i can't wait for my dues to be done
freedom is a feeling i feel coming
what a thought it is
that one day this life shall belong to me

twenty two
i realized i was surrounded by fools
everyone had the answers memorized
but no one knew what to do
i condensed my life into a backpack
and trusted my gut for the first time
life from here will be difficult
but it will never be boring again

twenty three
i've never felt so free
i got exactly what i wanted
but why am i the only person i know doing this
the loneliness
the overwhelmingness
on most days
i have no idea what i'm doing
but i really think
this is where i'm meant to be

twenty four
the unknown doesn't faze me anymore
there is this burning desire
of wanting my life to be so much more
i think i'm ready to commit
i want to do something big
the road ahead is uncertain
but i hope i'll be able to find it

twenty five
the world is taking a dive
there is this new virus it seems like
and i feel like i've been deprived
of what makes me feel alive
people are telling me to take it easy
maybe this year
will just be about trying to survive

twenty six
waiting for the world to be fixed
why the fuck am i still waiting
this irrational fear makes me sick
fuck it
one more one way ticket
i've decided
i don't want to live back home
ever again

twenty seven
i've completely lost my momentum
once again
i'm not sure where i'm headed
the last two years
i've been so caught up with trying to survive
it seems like i've lost my drive
i need to find my way back
to what makes me feel alive

twenty eight
i have made peace with my fate
it took me a while
but i found my way back to my path
i understand now
that i'm meant to live a life i create
if i keep going at this rate
i can still make it great

twenty nine
things are turning out fine
i got what i wanted
and my life is no longer a straight line
i am still learning how to shine
but i truly believe that everything will align
if i could keep letting this life
be mine

twenty something

i am still not
where i want to be
but i am glad things are not
what they used to be

do you ever look back at a spontaneous decision and think – *wow thank god i did that.*

it didn't seem like such a fine choice back then. people looked at you skeptically when you told them about your idea. you know they were secretly talking about you after you made your decision. their intentions probably weren't bad, but there were times where it did feel like the people whom you thought were on your side were secretly rooting for you to fail.

you didn't know what you were doing back then. most of your decisions were mostly just a feeling. pick up the things that give you energy. drop the things that make you feel like shit.

the first few steps were terribly confusing. you were just walking. you had no idea which direction you were going. and then somewhere along the way, something clicked.

you finally understand that this path you're walking on is the path you were always meant to be on. and thank god you took that leap.

twenty something

i'm a little bolder now at twenty nine
than i was at twenty five
i think more about what i think
than what people think of me

i've tried and i've failed
got a few successes out of what i do
on my best days i look at rejections
and i don't feel a thing

i still doubt myself
i don't think that really goes away
i'm still easily influenced by people
it's tricky finding the right ones
to surround yourself with

i've learned that good and bad
is mostly a made up concept
it's all relative to who you ask
i try not to get too caught up
trying to please both sides

i still don't know what i want
and i still wonder if i'll figure it out
i've been going on for a while now
what's a few more steps gonna do?

twenty something

some of the things
that didn't work out
turned out to be
the best things for me

my twenties are coming to an end.

it's an interesting feeling. the past decade has been the most life changing period of my life yet.

mentally, i feel a lot older than i am. i've done more than i ever thought i would, but still, i always feel like i could have done more.

it is never enough, is it?

i understand a lot more things now. why it worked, why it didn't. i don't really blame anyone other than myself.

i know i can't have everything, and i no longer try to.

at this point, age is just a number. i still have the rest of my life ahead of me, just like everyone else.

the older i get, the more i realize that we are all really the same.

we are all just trying to figure it out.

twenty something

if i made it here
i can probably
make it anywhere

thank you for reading to the end.

at the time of me writing this, i'm still in my twenties. it feels weird saying this, but i might not be by the time you read this.

looking back on the beginning of my twenties, the best thing i could have asked of myself was to spend it traveling, meeting lots of people all over the world, and trying out all my ideas.

i think i did exactly that.

most of it wasn't perfect. there were moments where my self doubt was so strong that it took me a long time to do very simple things. there were moments where i gave into my emotions and had higher expectations than i should have and spent too much time dwelling on my disappointments.

i want to say "if only i didn't do this or i didn't do that", but life doesn't work like that. without those mistakes, i might have never gotten to where i am today.

now that i'm at the end of my twenties, i can honestly say that i have no regrets about how i spent them. despite how reckless or insensible some of my decisions looked back then. i truly believe we mostly regret the things we didn't do.

growing up, i was never much of a writer. i started writing a lot in my twenties. mostly to cope with my journey.

i was traveling so much. always in a different place. always with different people. there were plenty of moments where i had a lot to say, but no one to say it to.

instagram became my outlet whenever i had something to say. and because of it, i was able to connect with people who had lives similar to mine. i think that saved my life.

it's a huge blessing to be able to do this. live my life. write about it. i hope i can continue to keep doing it.

i had so much fun writing this. i hope you enjoyed reading it.

i can't wait to hear what you think.

ron

p.s. there are 2 things you can do that would mean the world to me.

1. leave me a review on Amazon. or wherever you bought this. just write down what you think. it will help a lot more than you know.

2. if you take any pictures of my book to post on social media, tag me on @ronwritings. let people know where you got it.

ok signing off. bye!

Also by Ron Lim,

no idea what I'm doing but f*ck it